Artificial Intelligence in Healthcare

Sumit Das
Manas Kumar Sanyal

Artificial Intelligence in Healthcare

Intelligent Techniques for Medical Diagnosis

LAP LAMBERT Academic Publishing

Imprint

Any brand names and product names mentioned in this book are subject to trademark, brand or patent protection and are trademarks or registered trademarks of their respective holders. The use of brand names, product names, common names, trade names, product descriptions etc. even without a particular marking in this work is in no way to be construed to mean that such names may be regarded as unrestricted in respect of trademark and brand protection legislation and could thus be used by anyone.

Cover image: www.ingimage.com

Publisher:
LAP LAMBERT Academic Publishing
is a trademark of
International Book Market Service Ltd., member of OmniScriptum Publishing Group
17 Meldrum Street, Beau Bassin 71504, Mauritius

Printed at: see last page
ISBN: 978-620-0-78734-7

Copyright © Sumit Das, Manas Kumar Sanyal
Copyright © 2020 International Book Market Service Ltd., member of OmniScriptum Publishing Group

Artificial Intelligence in Healthcare:
Intelligent Techniques for Medical Diagnosis

Contents

Chapter 1	Medical Diagnosis	Page No.
1.1	Introduction Medical Diagnosis	5
1.2	Steps of Diagnosis	7
1.3	Introduction to Prediction	9
1.4	Prediction Techniques	9
Chapter 2	Artificial Intelligence in Medical Diagnosis	12
2.1	Introduction to Artificial Intelligence	12
2.2	2.2 Major components of AI	13
2.3	Types of Artificial Intelligence	15
2.4	AI techniques	16
2.5	First Oder Predicate Logic (FOPL)	19
2.6	Knowledge Representation	20
Chapter 3	AI programming in Medical Diagnosis	21
3.1	AI Programming	21
3.2	Introduction to PROLOG	22
3.3	Introduction to R	24
Chapter 4	AR and VR in Medical Diagnosis	26
Chapter 5	AI application in Medical Diagnosis	31
Chapter 6	Blockchain in Medical Diagnosis	35
Chapter 7	3D Printing in Healthcare	39
Chapter 8	References	41

Preface

This book is projected for the researchers/ students those who are want to work with AI in the field of healthcare and medical diagnosis. Specially, the researchers/ students want to model an AI machine, which acts as like Doctor, or expert system. This book covers the entire gamut of Artificial Intelligence particularly in the field of healthcare, medical diagnosis and intelligent treatment techniques. AI is the branch of computer science and information technology that deal with the real world computing by imitating the philosophy of human intelligence. In this book, authors try to illustrate the AI techniques that are being used for healthcare management. Authors also cite the prospect of healthcare using the advancement of Artificial Intelligence (AI) such as Machine Learning (ML), blockchain, 3D printing, Augmented Reality (AR) and Virtual Reality (VR).

The purpose of this book is to introduce AI techniques and its recent applications in medical diagnosis. The first chapter introduces the philosophy behind medical diagnosis that enables to find the pathway to model machine intelligent doctors. The prediction techniques are also discussed in this chapter. Chapter 2 illustrates the origin and the basic concept of AI. This chapter categories the type of AI and classify the subfields of it. The knowledge representation techniques are the basic concept of medical diagnosis also discussed here, which provide the knowledge base to the machine. The chapter 3 introduces the different AI programming languages for coding the real world knowledge base into machine for acquiring intelligent behavior. AR and VR technology discussed in chapter 4 which provide the artificially-real conceptual knowledge base to the practitioner to perform almost errorless diagnosis and treatment. The different applications are mentioned in chapter 5 to enable state of the art for future researches. The most recent new technology BLOCKCHAIN and 3D PRINTING are briefly introduce in chapter 6 and chapter 7 respectively. The blockchain speculates that it has the ability to perform secure and unambiguous diagnosis. Finally, 3D printing technologies provide the artificial organs to the practitioners as per requirement and provide sufficient information prior to take any sensitive decisions.

Acknowledgement

This book is a result of the collaborative efforts of many Scientists cited here. We express thank and gratitude each of them. We express our sense of gratitude to our students whose exceptional interactions have kept us alive intellectually and spiritually, to think and write. Our special thanks to our Management, JIS College of Engineering, JIS GROUP for encouragement as well as providing all kinds of required resources and facilities.

Sumit Das is presently working as an Asst. Professor in the Department of Information Technology, JIS College of Engineering, Kalyani, West Bengal, India.

Manas Kumar Sanyal is presently working as a Professor in the Department of Business Administration, former HOD, and Dean, faculty of Engineering, Technology and Management (ETM), University of Kalyani, West Bengal, India.

CHAPTER-1: Medical Diagnosis

1.1 Introduction

The nature of a disease and the identification of an illness are termed as diagnosis. It is the identification of any problem. The word diagnosis comes directly from the Greek, but the meaning has been changed. To the Greeks a diagnosis meant a "discrimination, a distinguishing, or a discerning among possibilities." Any practitioners his/her decision is acquired by diagnosis.

Disease Prevention & Health Promotion: Treatment depends on troublesome basic behavioral changes, as well as alterations in diet, taking over exercise, dropping smoking, cutting down drinking, and adhering to medication regimens that are typically complicated. The medical interview is used to collect information to assist in diagnosis, to understand patient values, to assess and communicate prognosis, to establish a therapeutic relationship, and to achieve agreement with the patient regarding additional diagnostic procedures and therapeutic choices. It serves as an opportunity to influence patient behavior, such as in motivational discussions about smoking cessation or medication adherence. Interviewing techniques that avoid domination by the practitioner increase patient involvement in care and patient satisfaction. Effective clinician-patient communication and enhanced patient involvement will improve health outcomes. Adherence may be a drawback in each practice; up to five hundredth of patients fails to realize full adherence, and third never take their medicines. Many patients with medical issues, even those with access to worry, do not seek appropriate care or may drop out of care prematurely. Studies show that over 60% of patients are less than 90% adherent and that adherence tends to decrease over time. Patient reasons for non-adherence embody easy forgetfulness, being far from home, being busy, and changes in daily routine. Other reasons include psychiatric disorders, uncertainty about the effectiveness of treatment, lack of knowledge about the consequences of poor adherence, regimen complexity, and treatment side effects. The rising costs of medications, including generic drugs, and the increase in patient cost-sharing burden, has made adherence even more difficult, for those with lower incomes. Patients appear higher ready to take prescribed medications than to stick to recommendations to alter their diet, exercise habits, or alcohol intake or to perform numerous self-care activities. For short-run regimens, adherence to medications can be improved by giving clear instructions. Writing out recommendation to patients, together with changes in medication, could also be useful. Because low functional health literacy is common, other forms of communication—such as illustrated simple text, videotapes, or oral instructions—may be more effective[1].

Common Symptoms: Evidence-based symptom analysis combines information of a symptom's clinical medicine with illness candidates in step with Bayesian principles, such the probability of a particular illness may be a function of patient demographics, co-morbidities, and clinical features. This knowledge supports decisions about further testing, or treatment or whether to perform additional testing before treatment. Biological, psychological, social, and cultural factors affect how patients experience, interpret, and describe symptoms, and whether their symptoms are sufficiently bothersome or worrisome to seek medical attention. Host and environmental factors can influence the symptoms that are manifested.

In 1967, Evans planned 5 "realities" that replicate the problem clinicians face once associating associate acute metabolism syndrome with associate etiologic pathogen:
(1) A similar clinical syndrome could also be made by a spread of infectious agents;
(2) An equivalent pathogen could turn out a spread of syndromes;
(3) The foremost probably reason behind a syndrome could vary by patient age, year, geography, and setting;
(4) Diagnosing of the infectious agent is often not possible on the premise of clinical findings alone; and
(5) the causes of an oversized proportion of communicable disease syndromes are still unknown[2].

Preoperative Evaluation & Perioperative Management: Operative mortality and morbidity have declined due to improvements in surgical, anesthetic, and monitoring techniques. The traditional preoperative roles of the medical consultant or primary care provider include evaluating the severity and stability of medical conditions, assessing the risk of medical complications, determining whether further preoperative risk stratification testing is indicated, and recommending measures to reduce the risk of perioperative complications. The consultant may be asked to manage medical aspects of patients' postoperative care, including evaluation and treatment of medical complications. Patients while not vital medical problems—especially those below age 50—are at terribly low risk for perioperative complications. Their preoperative evaluation should include a history and physical examination. Special stress is placed on getting a careful medicine history and assessment of practical standing, exercise tolerance, and respiratory organ symptoms and signs in an endeavor to reveal antecedently unrecognized malady that may require further evaluation prior to surgery[3].

Diagnostic Testing & Medical Decision Making: The clinician's main task is to make reasoned decisions about patient care based on available clinical information and estimated clinical outcomes1. To determine check sensitivity and specificity for a specific illness, the test must be compared against an independent "gold standard" test or established standard diagnostic criteria that define the true disease state of the patient. The utility of a check in a very explicit clinical scenario depends not solely on the check's characteristics however on the likelihood that the patient has the illness before the test result is known. Likelihood Ratios (LR) combine both test sensitivity and specificity into a single measure, which helps evaluate and interpret a diagnostic test. Likelihood ratios provide an estimation of whether there will be significant change in pretest to posttest probability of a disease given the test result, and can be used to make quick estimates of the utility of contemplated diagnostic tests above all things. To estimate the potential benefit of a diagnostic test, the clinician first estimates the pretest odds of disease given all available clinical information and multiplies the pretest odds by the positive and negative likelihood ratios.

Use of a diagnostic assay is bonded once its result may shift the likelihood of illness across the treatment threshold. The approach is in keeping with the rapidly evolving field of personalized medicine, in which diagnostic testing plays an important role in selecting the best possible therapies that are tailored to individual characteristics of each patient. Computerized clinical decision support systems, along with test order communication systems, have been increasingly used to develop, implement, and refine computerized protocols for specific processes of care derived from evidence-based practice guidelines[4].

1.2 Steps of Diagnosis

The steps of the diagnostic method fall under 3 broad categories:

1) Initial Diagnostic Assessment – Patient history, physical examination, analysis of the patient's chief criticism and symptoms, forming a medical diagnosis, and ordering of diagnostic tests
2) Diagnostic Testing – Performance, interpretation, and communication of test results
3) Referral, Consultation, Treatment & Follow-Up – Physician follow-up, referrals and consults, discharge process and patient compliance

The flow of diagnostic process[5] as shown in figure 1:

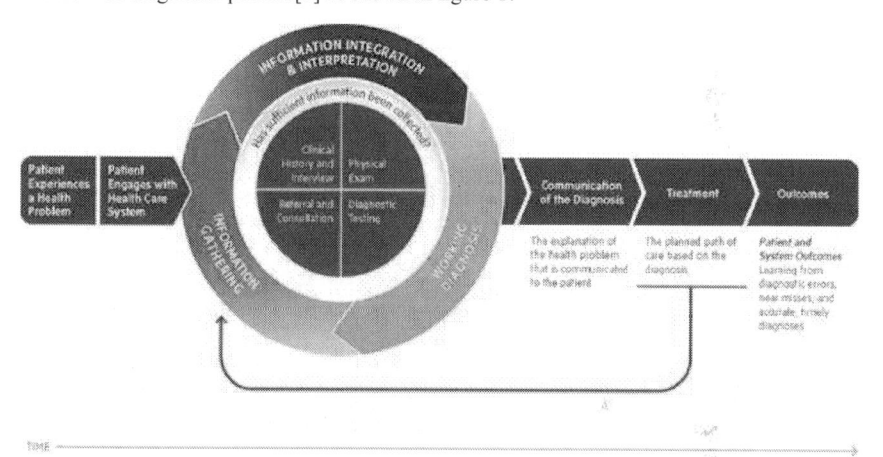

Fig 1. The Flow of Diagnosis

The persistent drawback of diagnostic error mandates that the authors take the time to larn the diagnostic method in conjunction with the system and psychological feature errors that usually occur at every stage. Avoidance of medical mistakes starts with awareness, education and meta-cognition, followed by sustainable changes in those clinical behaviors that improve diagnostic performance and reduce errors. The 2015 report from the Institute of Medicine, "Improving Diagnosis in Health Care," has outlined a model of the diagnostic process, as has CRICO Strategies in its "2014 Annual Benchmarking Report." each models describe the ten to twelve parts that comprise the method and discuss the inadequacies and errors that will plague every step. Of particular interest is the data from CRICO that analyzed over 2,300 malpractice cases and determined the frequency of error associated with each step in the diagnostic process. It is at this stage where a misdiagnosis often starts - when a clinician fails to carefully listen and elicit a thorough history that includes all medications, surgeries, medical conditions, family and social history. The step is to integrate the information gathered from the chief complaint, history, exam and risk factors into a differential diagnosis. This phase of the diagnostic process is arguably the most critical because errors that occur during the earlier steps are compounded and result in a differential diagnosis that is either too narrow or off target. Mistakes in judgment created at now will serve to derail the whole diagnostic method, and unless a disciplined redirection happens down the road, the proper identification could also be delayed or missed, with serious consequences to the patient's outcome and safety. More malpractice cases involve errors at the differential diagnosis step (33% of cases) than at any other step in the process, with errors in test ordering coming in a close second (30%). The IOM report, while pointing out that there is no single solution, listed 8 "Goals for Improving Diagnosis and Reducing Diagnostic Error," with an emphasis on education and training for all healthcare professionals in areas deemed to be deficient, including clinical reasoning, teamwork, communication, and the use of diagnostic testing and health IT. A good place for clinicians to start is to revisit the diagnostic process and carefully dissect each step to reveal not only its benefits, but the hazards that lead to errors along the way[5], [6] as shown in figure 2.

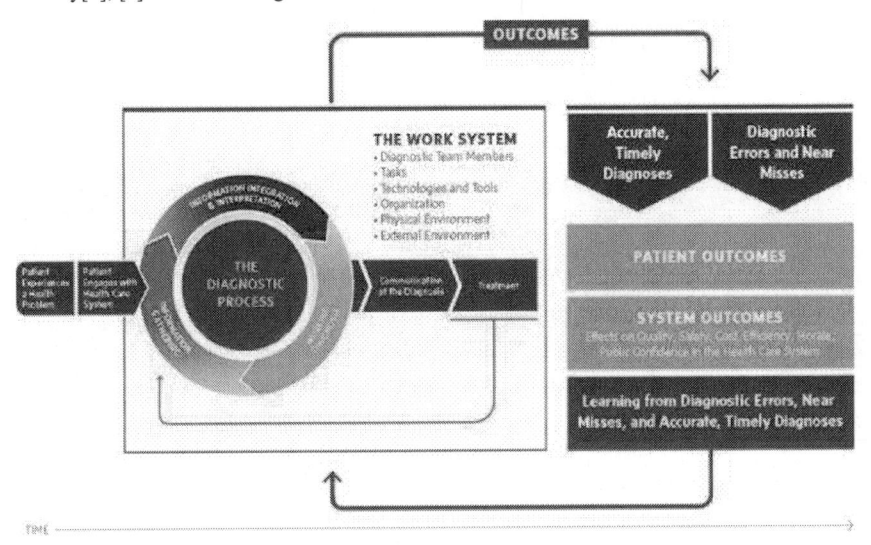

Fig 2. The outcome of diagnosis

Steps to Reduce Evaluation and Cognitive Errors:

1) Employ decision support algorithms, to manage both screening and symptomatic patients.
2) Use electronic decision support tools such as the Isabel Differential Diagnosis (DDx) Generator to help build differential diagnosis lists and rule in or rule out potentially serious conditions.
3) Use general and symptom-based checklists to help rule in or rule out potentially serious conditions. The Society to Improve Diagnosis in Medicine (SIDM) offers several.

4) Maintain a high state of alertness for patients who return with unresolved or worsening complaints. Broaden the differential diagnosis list. Seek a second opinion if necessary.
5) Encourage patients to become informed and activated, to ask questions and advocate on their behalf. Patients can use the National Patient Safety Foundation's Checklist for Getting the Right Diagnosis.

The AI system is completely depended on the philosophy of how the human beings are doing the task. In case of medical diagnosis, the physicians' follows the steps of medical diagnosis and in the same way if anyone wants to develop AI medical diagnostic system, the same step have to be followed in logical manner. The above sections have been discussed for the reference of the reader for acquiring the preliminary knowledgebase of medical diagnosis that enable you to get the logical flow (knowledgebase) of medical diagnosis as like a physician.

1.3 Introduction to Prediction

Prediction is defined as the outcome or result of an algorithm whenever the algorithm was trained with historical data. When a new data is taken as input to the trained algorithm, it forecast the probable output. Machine learning algorithms are programs that can learn from data and improve from experience, without human intervention. Learning objective might embody learning the task that maps the input to the output, learning the hidden structure in untagged data; or 'instance-based learning', wherever a category label is created for a new instance by comparing the new instance to instances from the training data, which were stored in memory. The doctor also performs diagnosis by incorporating prediction techniques and there are some likelihood in the outcome of it. Therefore, the Artificial Intelligence Doctor (AIDr)[7], [8] could be modeled using the logical consequence of physician' diagnosis philosophy.

1.4 Prediction Techniques

The prediction techniques refer to Machine Learning (ML) algorithms such as supervised learning, unsupervised learning and ensemble technique.

Supervised learning is the technique in which input and output variable are presented. The algorithm is trained with labeled data and the learning mode is offline. This learning simply mapped input data: x to output: f(x).

The common supervised learning techniques:

- ✓ *Regression-* It is the technique to find the relation between one dependent variable and one or more independent variables. Regression between one dependent variable and one independent variable is known as linear regression. Regression between one dependent variable and two or more independent variables are known as multiple regressions.
- ✓ *Logistic Regression-* In linear regression the dependent variable is always a continuous variable. The dependent variable was categorical, you cannot use linear regression model it. Logistic regression can be used to model and solve such problems, called as binary classification problems. Logistic regression is a classic predictive modeling technique and remains a popular choice for modeling binary categorical variables.

- ✓ *Classification and Regression Trees (CART)* - It refers to Decision Tree algorithms that can be used for classification or regression predictive modeling problems. The CART algorithm provides a foundation for bagged decision trees, random forest and boosted decision trees.
- ✓ *Naïve Bayes-* Naive Bayes model on the entire dataset and making a single prediction for a new observation. Bayes' Theorem provides a way that we can calculate the probability of a piece of data belonging to a given class, given our prior knowledge. Naive Bayes is a classification algorithm for binary (two-class) and multiclass classification problems. It is called Naive Bayes or idiot Bayes because the calculations of the probabilities for each class are simplified to make their calculations tractable.
- ✓ *K-Nearest Neighbors (KNN)* - It is the technique used for distance calculation and locate neighbors within a dataset. Neighbors for a new piece of data in the dataset are the k closest instances, as defined by the distance measure.

Whereas, unsupervised learning is the technique in which only input variable are presented. The input data are not labeled but the learning mode is real time.

The common unsupervised learning techniques:

- ✓ *K-means-* A cluster refers to a collection of data points aggregated together because of certain similarities. Every data point is allocated to each of the clusters through reducing the in-cluster sum of squares. The K-means algorithm identifies k number of centroids, and allocates every data point to the nearest cluster, while keeping the centroids as small as possible. The 'means' in the K-means refers to averaging of the data; that is, finding the centroid. To process the learning data, the K-means algorithm in data mining starts with a first group of randomly selected centroids, which are used as the beginning points for every cluster, and performs iterative calculations to optimize the positions of the centroids.
- ✓ *Principal Component Analysis (PCA)-* PCA is a simple dimensionality reduction technique that transforms the columns of a dataset into a new set features called Principal Components (PCs). The primary objective of Principal Components is to represent the information in the dataset with minimum columns possible.

Ensembling learning is the technique of combing the outcome of multiple learners. This technique used averaging at regression and voting at classification for improving the outcome of ensembling.

The common ensembling learning techniques:

- ✓ *Bagging with Random Forests-* Bagging(Bootstrap Aggregation) is the application of the Bootstrap procedure to a high-variance machine learning algorithm, typically decision trees. Random Forests are an improvement over bagged decision trees. Random forest changes the algorithm for the way that the sub-trees are learned so that the resulting predictions from all of the subtrees have less correlation.
- ✓ Boosting with XGBoost(extream gradient boosting)- The gradient can be used to find the direction in which to change the model parameters in order to reduce the error in the round of training by "descending the gradient". XGBoost stands for Extreme Gradient Boosting; it is a specific implementation of the Gradient Boosting method which uses

more accurate approximations to find the best tree model. While regular gradient boosting uses the loss function of the base model as a proxy for minimizing the error of the overall model, XGBoost uses the 2nd order derivative as an approximation.

The reader can use these techniques to model and implement an AI system for medical diagnosis[9], which may not required direct intervention of physicians.

CHAPTER-2: Artificial Intelligence in Medical Diagnosis

2.1 Introduction to Artificial Intelligence

Artificial Intelligence (AI) is termed as the techniques to build intelligent machine that can recognize speech, detect object, solve problem, learn from given data and plan for task to be done.

The term AI first coined by Jone McCarthy in 1956 and then Shakey in 1969 built the first general purpose ROBOT. In 1997, the first supercomputer 'DEEP BLUE' was built which was defeat the World Chess champion in a game. Finally, the first commercially robotic vacuum clinker created in 2002 and now onwards people are having the application of AI in every aspect in daily life as shown in figure 3.

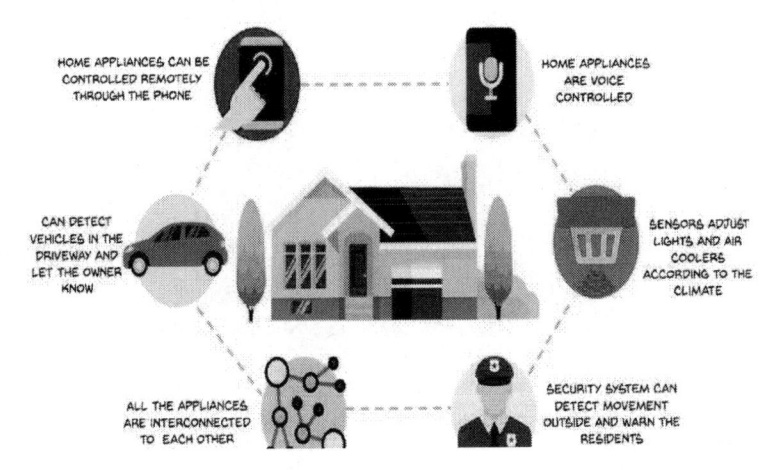

Fig.3 AI in daily life.

The human intelligence refers to the ability to acquire and apply different skills, knowledge to solve a given problem. Now, in this advance digital era, intelligence involves both Human and Artificial Intelligence. The critical human intelligence is concerned with solving problems, reasoning and learning.

AI is about artificial creativity to begin the end of innovation. The content automation tool such as wordsmith-generate written analytics by translating given data. In Social media, AI is used for face verification and machine learning (ML), deep learning (DL) used for detecting facial features. Here also, AI through NLP identifies hate speech and terrorist activities. Amazon Echo

Alexa is a device used to perform various real life tasks by using command. It also used AI and ML for recommendation of product. NETFLIX recommended movie through AI, ML and DL. Google assistance used AI to process natural language and perform tasks through conversation with it. TESLA self-driving car is an autonomous vehicle is the outcome of AI trough image detection and deep learning. Healthcare: IBM Watson used AI for medical diagnosis.

2.2 Major components of AI

AI is broad branch of Computer Science (CS) and Information Technology (IT), enables the machine to think and function intelligently & independently. AI works two ways:
   a. Symbolic learning, which is completely symbolic-based and it is relay on image processing techniques.
   b. Machine learning (ML) which is completely data-based.

ML provides statistical tool to explore the data. The ML techniques are supervised learning, unsupervised learning and reinforcement/ semi supervised learning. The supervise learning is applied in the field where prediction is the main objective and unsupervised learning is concerned with classification. The reinforcement learning applied in the field where the outcome is the function of trial and errors. Computer vision and robotics is the outcome of symbolic learning.

Deep learning (DL) is multi-neural network architecture, which mimic human brain. The DL classified as
   a. Artificial Neural Network (ANN) which takes the input data as numbers,
   b. Convolution Neural Network(CNN) which takes the input data as image,
   c. Recurrent Neural Network (RNN), which takes the input as time series data.

Data Science (DS) encompasses most of the AI techniques as shown in figure 4(a) and it acquires intelligence by using the tools such as statistics, probability and linear algebra. Speech recognition is used statistical theory and it is called statistical learning (SL). The Natural Language processing (NLP) & speech recognition is the outcome SL.

The grouping of like object is known as the pattern recognition and it is the field of ML. Cognitive capability in machine is acquired by ANN, and it is modeled by mimicking the human brain. More complex ANN models are termed as the deep learning network. In computer vision, the object is recognized by CNN and o remembers the limited past the computer uses RNN. In addition to ANN, the fuzzy logic (FL) and genetic algorithms (Gas) are important components of cognitive science, which belongs to AI. That ANN, FL and GAs are the basic constituent of Soft Computing (SC).

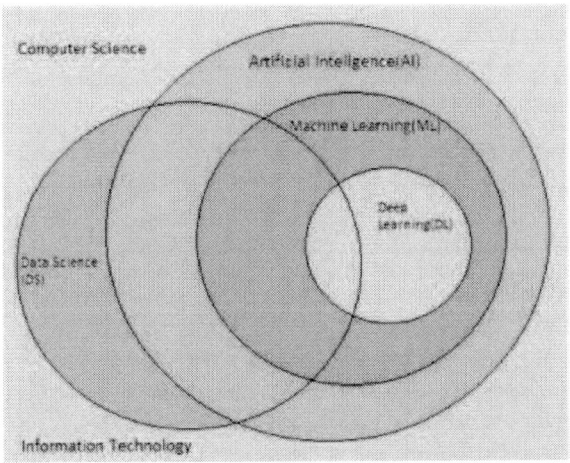

Fig.4. (a) Components of AI

The Sub-fields of AI as shown in figure 4(b) are Neural Networks, Evolutionary Computation, Vision, Robotics, Expert Systems, Speech Processing, Planning, Machine Learning, and NLP. Scientific Goal to work out which ideas about knowledge representation, learning, rule systems, search, and so on, explain various forms of real intelligence. Engineering Goal to resolve real-world problems using AI techniques like knowledge representation, learning, rule systems, search, and so on.

Artificial Intelligence has identifiable roots during a very number of older disciplines, Philosophy Logic/Mathematics Computation Psychology/Cognitive Science Biology/Neuroscience Evolution. Many sub-fields of AI are simultaneously building models of how the human system operates, and artificial systems for solving real-world problems, and are allowing useful ideas to transfer between them. Artificial neural networks perform well at many simple tasks and supply good models of the many human abilities. AI consist many sub-fields, using a variety of techniques, such as[10]

- Neural Networks – e.g. brain modeling, statistic prediction, classification
- Evolutionary Computation – e.g. genetic algorithms, genetic programming
- Computer Vision – e.g. object recognition, image understanding
- Robotics – e.g. intelligent control, autonomous exploration
- Expert Systems – e.g. decision support systems, teaching systems and FL control
- Speech Processing– e.g. speech recognition and production
- NLP Processing – e.g. machine translation
- Planning – e.g. scheduling, game playing
- Machine Learning – e.g. decision tree learning, version space learning

Major sub-fields of AI include Machine Learning, Neural Networks, Evolutionary Computation, Vision, Robotics, Expert Systems, Speech Processing, NLP Processing, and Planning. Major common techniques used across many of these sub-fields include Knowledge Representation, Rule Systems, Search and Learning.

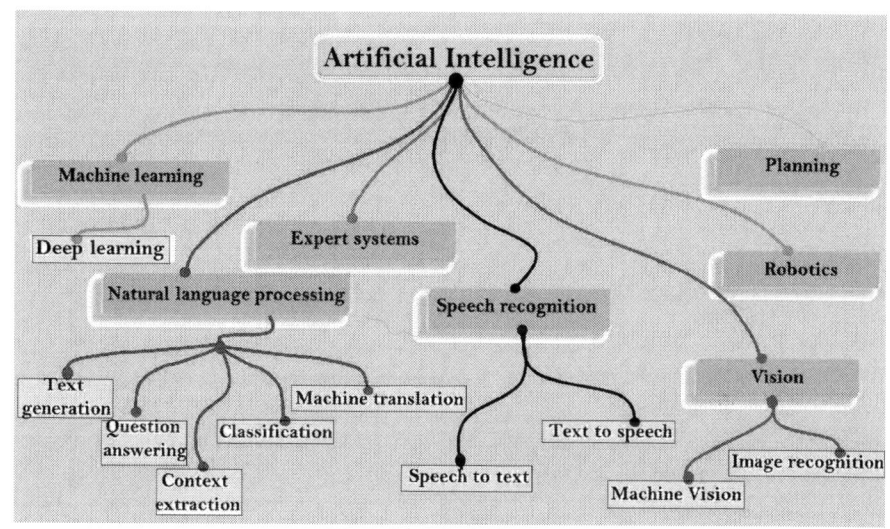

Fig.4. (b) Sub-fields of AI

2.3 Types of Artificial Intelligence

There are two types of artificial intelligence: type-1 and type-2 AI.

Type-1 AI falls in three categories based on the stages:

a) Artificial Narrow Intelligence (ANI) - It is designed to perform specific tasks without self-expand functionality. For example today's intelligent automation such as self-driving, medical diagnosis, financial advice and so on. The ANI enhanced the jobs market.
b) Artificial General Intelligence (AGI) - It is being designed to perform broad tasks and will have the reason, improve capabilities comparable to humans. The implication is that AGI will cause the jobs at risk in 2040.
c) Artificial Super Intelligence (ASI) – It will have the intelligence beyond the humans' capabilities. The implication is that ASI will cause the humans at risk as it outperforms them. It will appear after AGI.

Type-2 AI falls into the following four categories based on the functionalities:
   a) Reactive machines- It has no memory and only responds to current different stimuli. The most basic types of AI systems are purely reactive, and have the ability neither to form memories nor to use past experiences to advise current decisions. Deep Blue, IBM's chess-playing supercomputer, which beat international grandmaster Garry Kasparov in the late 1990s, is the perfect example of this type of machine.
   b) Limited memory- It uses memory to learn and improve responses. The limited memory AI contains machines that can look into the past. For example, the observations are added to the self-driving cars' preprogrammed representations of the world, which also include lane markings, traffic lights and other important elements, like curves in the road.
   c) Theory of mind- It understands other intelligent entities and tries to responds. Psychology tells us that people have thoughts, emotions, memories, and mental models that drive their behavior. Theory of mind AI researchers hopes to build computers that imitate people's mental models, by forming representations about the world, other agents and entities in it.
   d) Self-awareness- It is stuff of science fiction, though many AI enthusiasts believe them to be the ultimate goal of AI development. In self-awareness-AI, scientists are trying to creating machines that are self-aware, and they are focusing the efforts toward understanding memory, learning and the ability to take decisions on experiences.

2.4 AI Techniques for Medical Diagnosis

The researchers are increasingly looking into new and innovative techniques with the help of information technology to overcome the rapid surge in healthcare costs facing the community. Research has shown that artificial intelligence (AI) tools and techniques can aid in the diagnosis of disease states and assessment of treatment outcomes. This has been demonstrated in a number of areas, including: help with medical decision support system. The classification of heart disease acquired from electrocardiogram (ECG) waveforms. The identification of epileptic seizure from electroencephalogram (EEG) signals. The ophthalmology to detect glaucoma disease, abnormality in movement pattern recognition for rehabilitation and potential falls risk minimization, assisting functional electrical stimulation (FES) control in rehabilitation setting of spinal cord injured patients, and clustering of medical images[11].

Effective networking between informatics and biomedical engineering can help to complement each other's knowledge and to fight in partnership the various challenges faced by the medical and healthcare systems. Artificial Intelligence Techniques such as neural networks, Fuzzy logic, Support vector machines, Genetic algorithms and Machine Learning are the most common techniques for medical diagnosis. The applications of AI have the potential to influence how clinicians and health care systems approach diagnostics and the ability for individuals to understand changes to their health in real-time.

With projected rapid growth in the medical device sector, companies making efforts to bring accurate and reliable medical diagnostics based on machine and deep learning applications to market may be poised to capture a percentage of this profitable market.

Many of today's machine learning diagnostic applications appear to fall under the following categories[12]:

- ✓ Chat-bots: Companies are using AI-chatbots with speech recognition capability to identify patterns in patient symptoms to form a potential diagnosis, prevent disease and/or recommend an appropriate course of action.

Here the programmer converts the words in the sentence pairs to their corresponding indexes from the vocabulary and feed this to the models. If the programmer converts the English sentences to tensors by converting words to their indexes and zero-pad, the tensor would have shape and indexing the first dimension would return a full sequence across all time-steps. The programmer transposes the input batch shape to, so that indexing across the first dimension returns a time step across all sentences in the batch. The second RNN is a decoder, which takes an input word and the context vector, and returns a guess for the word in the sequence and a hidden state to use in the iteration[13].

- ✓ Oncology: Researchers are using deep learning to train algorithms to recognize cancerous tissue at a level comparable to trained physicians. (Readers with a specific focus on cancer treatments may be interested in reading our full article on deep learning in oncology.)

Knowledge often comes from multiple sources and must be integrated. These sources may not have the same division of the world. The people involved in designing a knowledge base must choose what individuals and relationships to represent. Different people involved in a knowledge-based system should agree on this division of the world. RDF (Resource Description Framework) is a language built on XML, providing individual-property-value triples. RDF-S lets you restrict the domain and range of properties and provides containers. OWL (Web Ontology Language) is an ontology language for the World Wide Web. It defines some classes and properties with a fixed interpretation that can be used for describing classes, properties, and individuals. People who want to develop a knowledge base can use an existing ontology or develop their own ontology, usually built on existing ontologies. A conceptualization for small knowledge bases can be in the head of the designer or specified in natural language in the documentation[14].

In AI, an ontology is a specification of the meanings of the symbols in an information system. The objective of using ontology are to share common understanding of the structure of information among people or software agents, enable reuse of domain knowledge, make domain assumptions explicit, separate domain knowledge from the operational knowledge and analyze domain knowledge [15]

An ontology may give axioms to restrict the use of some symbol. Ontologies are usually written independently of a particular application and often involve a community to agree on the meanings of symbols. An ontology is required to specify the meaning of the symbols for the user and to allow the knowledge bases to interoperate. The main challenge in building an ontology is the organization of the concepts to allow a human to map concepts into symbols in the computer, and for the computer to infer useful new knowledge from stated facts[16].

- ✓ Pathology: Pathology is the medical specialty that is concerned with the diagnosis of disease based on the laboratory analysis of bodily fluids such as blood and urine, as well as tissues. Machine vision and other machine learning technologies can enhance the efforts traditionally left only to pathologists with microscopes.

Electronic decision support is increasingly prevalent in clinical practice. Traditional tools map guidelines into an interactive platform. Machine learning allows computers to predict outcomes from data without being explicitly programmed. Hidden layers in the artificial neural network represent increasingly more complex features in the data. Convolutional Neural Networks (CNNs), a type of deep learning, are commonly used for image analysis -deep learning model example. An approach to diagnosis that incorporates multiple sources of raw data. It extracts biologically and clinically relevant information from these data. It uses mathematic models at the molecular, individual, and population levels to generate diagnostic inferences and predictions. It also presents this clinically actionable knowledge to customers through dynamic and integrated reports and interfaces, enabling physicians, patients, laboratory personnel, and other health care system stakeholders to make the best possible medical decisions. A digital camera captures the same field of view (FoV) as the user and passes the image to an attached compute unit capable of running real-time inference of a machine-learning model. Computational pathology is coming with near term applications of narrow AI to clinical problems

The accelerated adoption of digital pathology in clinical practice has ushered in new horizons for both computer vision and AI. Because of recent success stories in image recognition for nonmedical applications, many researchers and entrepreneurs are convinced that AI in general and deep learning in particular may be able to assist with many tasks in digital pathology. A Pathology AI system with an intended use for clinical Diagnostics (Dx), Prognostics (Px) or Companion Diagnostics (CDx) can be commercialized under a central lab model either as a Lab Developed Test (LDT) or a single-site medical device. Pharmacy companies who want to bring their drugs to market and payers who want to improve patient care and lower healthcare costs need to provide a viable business model that is based on the value that is provided by pharma-co-genomics and big data[17].

- ✓ Rare Diseases: Facial recognition software is being combined with machine learning to help clinicians diagnose rare diseases. Patient photos are analyzed using facial analysis and deep learning to detect phenotypes that correlate with rare genetic diseases.

It is important to note that physician performance is typically not the direct cause of diagnostic errors. In fact, researchers attribute the cause of diagnostics errors to a variety of factors including:

- ✓ Inefficient collaboration and integration of health information technologies (Health IT)
- ✓ Gaps in communication among clinicians, patients and their families
- ✓ A healthcare work system which, by design, does not adequately support the diagnostic process

Machine Learning algorithms can learn to see patterns to the way doctors see them. Machine Learning is helpful in areas where the diagnostic information a doctor examines is already digitized. The application of Machine Learning in diagnostics is just beginning; systems that are more ambitious involve the combination of multiple data sources (CT, MRI, genomics and proteomics, patient data, and even handwritten files) in assessing a disease or its progression. Many of the analytical processes involved in drug development can be made more efficient with Machine Learning. Machine Learning can speed up the design of clinical trials by automatically identifying suitable candidates as well as ensuring the correct distribution for groups of trial participants. Algorithms can help identify patterns that separate good candidates from bad. They can serve as an early warning system for a clinical trial that is not producing conclusive results – allowing the researchers to intervene earlier, and potentially saving the development of the drug. Machine Learning can automate the complicated statistical work and help discover which characteristics indicate that a patient will have a particular response to a particular treatment.

2.5 First Order Predicate Logic (FOPL)

First-order logic (FOL) is precisely what's sometimes been thought of as "Good Old-Fashioned AI" (GOFAI) and what was the central target of critique on AI research coming from other fields like probabilistic reasoning and machine learning[18]. The basic elements of FOPL are as follows in table 1.

Table 1: Elements of FOPL[19]

Elements	Examples
Constant	1, 2, A, John, Mumbai, cat,….
Variables	x, y, z, a, b,….
Predicates	Brother, Father, >,….
Function	sqrt, LeftLegOf, ….
Connectives	$\wedge, \vee, \neg, \Rightarrow, \Leftrightarrow$
Equality	==
Quantifier	$\forall, \exists$

FOL inference will be done by: propositionalize KB and query, apply resolution, and return result. Example: ∀ x King(x) ∧ Greedy(x) ⇒ Evil(x) K ing(J ohn) ∀ y Greedy(y) Brother(Richard, John) propositionalization produces not only Greedy(John), but Greedy(Richard) which is irrelevant for a query Evil(John)

Therefore, the present state-of-the-art provides a series of unifications of probabilistic and first-order representations. I think this is often what makes it important to find out and understand first-order representations – which is best taught within the context of FOL. The reasoning and inference methods one requires recent relational probabilistic models are in fact different to classical logical reasoning. Therefore, it was knowing about "logical reasoning" is not so important than knowing about "logical representations". Still, some basic aspects of logical reasoning, like computing all possible substitutions for an abstract.

2.6 Knowledge Representation (KR)

The knowledgebase is a collection of Declarative knowledge and Procedural knowledge.

a) Declarative Knowledge (Knowledge Representation): It contains the description of notation, facts, and rules of the world. It is non-procedural, independent of targets, problem solving and tells about right or wrong.
b) Procedural Knowledge (Reasoning): Description of procedural required to achieve targets. It is a collection of rules, procedures and provides logical inference over the knowledge base.

The KR forms are divided into four categories, which are as follows:

a) Network-Based Representation: Semantic network
b) Structure-Based Representation: Frame
c) Production Rule Representation
d) Logical Representation

Having reviewed various knowledge representation paradigms[20], it found that there are multiple different ways of approaching the representation of knowledge. The semantic network knowledge representation form is suitable for expressing the general statement and capturing the taxonomic structure. Semantic networks and frame are identical with respect to expressiveness but both uses different metaphors. Rule-based form of knowledge representation is appropriate for reasoning over instance data. Logical representation of the knowledge captures all the information about objects. You can convert semantic networks and rules into the logical knowledge representation form.

CHAPTER-3: AI Programming in Medical Diagnosis

3.1 AI Programming Languages

Programmer those who are working on an artificial intelligence project and still have not decided which language should use to program it. The following are the common AI programming languages. Among these one can use any one of that based on the model or working prototype[21].

Python is considered to be in the first place in the list of all AI development languages due to the simplicity. Many AI algorithms can be implemented in it. Python takes short development time in comparison to other languages like Java, C++ or Ruby. Functional as well as procedure oriented styles of programming. For example: Numpy is a library for python that helps them to solve many scientific computations. The package Pybrain that is for using machine learning in Python.

R is one of the most effective language and environment for analyzing and manipulating the data for statistical purposes. Apart from being a general purpose language, R has numerous of packages like RODBC, Gmodels, Class and Tm which are used in the field of machine learning. These packages make the implementation of machine learning algorithms easy, for cracking the business associated problems.

LISP is one of the oldest and the most suited languages for the development in AI. Its development cycle allows interactive evaluation of expressions and recompilation of functions or file while the program is still running. Due to advancement, many of these features have migrated into many other languages thereby affecting the uniqueness of

PROLOG is the language stays alongside Lisp when the authors talk about development in AI field. The features provided by it include efficient pattern matching, tree-based data structuring and automatic backtracking. All these features provide a surprisingly powerful and flexible programming framework. Prolog is widely used for working on medical projects and for designing expert AI systems.

Java provides many benefits: easy use, debugging ease, package services, simplified work with large-scale projects, graphical representation of data and better user interaction. Artificial intelligence has lot to do with search algorithms, artificial neural networks and genetic programming.

3.2 Introduction to PROLOG

Programming in Logic (PROLOG) is termed as a logic-based programming language. The programs correspond to sets of logical formulas and the Prolog interpreter uses logical methods to resolve queries. Prolog is a declarative language. The programmer specifies what problem you want to solve rather than how to solve it. Prolog is useful in the problem areas, such as artificial intelligence, natural language processing, databases, but not suitable for graphics or numerical algorithms. Prolog expressions are comprised of the subsequent truth-functional symbols, which have a similar interpretation as within the symbolic logic[22]. Following are the basic constituents of PROLOG programming:

Fact

A fact is a predicate expression that makes a declarative statement about the problem domain. Whenever a variable occurs during a Prolog expression, it's assumed to be universally quantified. All Prolog sentences must end with a period.

Example 1:

likes(ram, sita).   /* Ram likes Sita */
likes(sita, ram).   /* Sita likes Ram */
likes(X, sita).   /* Everyone likes Sita */
likes(ram, Y).   /* Ram likes everybody */
likes(ram, Y), likes(Y, ram).   /* Ram likes everybody and everybody likes Ram */
likes(ram, sita); likes(ram,maruti). /* Ram likes Sita or Ram likes Maruti*/
not(likes(ram,fruit)).   /* Ram does not like fruit */
likes(ram,sita) :- likes(ram,maruti). /* Ram likes Sita if Ram likes Maruti*/

Rule

A rule could be a predicate expression that uses logical relation (:-) to explain a relationship among facts. A Prolog rule takes the shape left_hand_side :- right_hand_side . This sentence is interpreted as: left_hand_side will be true if right_hand_side is true. The left_hand_side is restricted to one, positive, literal, which suggests it must contain a positive atomic expression. In Horn clause logic, the left side of the clause is that the conclusion, and must be one positive literal. The Horn clause calculus is like the first-order symbolic logic.

Example 2:
friends(X, Y) :- likes(X,Y),likes(Y,X).

Query

The prolog interpreter responds to queries about the facts and rules represented in its database. The database is assumed to represent what's true a few particular problem domains. In making a question, you're asking Prolog whether it can prove that your query is true. If so, it answers "yes" and displays any variable bindings that it made in arising with the solution. If it fails to prove the query true, it answers "No".

Example 3:
? friends(ram, sita).
True.

Prolog is a computer language that has aspects that make it different from such other languages as PL/I, Pascal, COBOL, or FORTRAN[23]. A Prolog program can be viewed as a set of logical axioms, where executing a Prolog establishes a proof that a certain desired conclusion follows from that set of axioms. Much attention is currently focused on expert-systems shells, which play a task in AI systems almost like that of application generators in additional conventional applications. The Prolog language embodies many of the features found in these shells while providing a comparatively general and complete language. When the intelligent agent implemented solely based on the logical rules system, it showed a competitive behavior at a medium level, executing the basic actions of winning, blocking and building in an accurate way; after many tests, the authors noticed that it was necessary to implement more rules through of case-based reasoning technique.

The healthcare domain may be a big and significant area where people, different organizations and various institutions get services still as provide services at constant time. The devices are capable enough to transmit vital signs data from a patient's home to the hospital staff, allowing them to possess real-time monitoring of the patient's health. These devices use wirelessly connected gluco-meters, scales, pulse rate, and pressure, monitors. The best feature of all these devices is the possibility to wear them, to have them monitoring the person who's wearing them 24/7. This diagnosis is implemented and supported by an underlying framework[24] that combines the most recent technologies that are changing the healthcare environment: IoT (Internet of Things) and Data Analytics. There are plenty of possibilities for improving the whole framework, e.g. using natural language processing to automatically instantiate the individuals in the DSO ontology, or extending the framework to new wearable devices.

3.3 Introduction to R

It includes machine learning algorithms, regression, statistic, statistical inference to call a couple of data analysis with R is completed during a series of steps; programming, transforming, discovering, modeling and communicating the results. The primary uses of R are always being in statistics, visualization, and machine learning. The picture below in figure 5 depicts the training curve compared to the business capability a language offers. If you want to give the best insight from the data, you need to spend some time learning the appropriate tool, which is R. Python could be a fantastic tool to deploy Machine Learning and AI but lacks communication features. With a consistent learning curve, R could be a good trade-off between implementation and data analysis. The best algorithms for machine learning will be implemented with R. Packages like Keras and TensorFlow[25] allow creating high-end machine learning techniques. Concisely, R could be a great tool to explore and investigate the information. Elaborate analyses like clustering, correlation, and data reduction are finished with R.

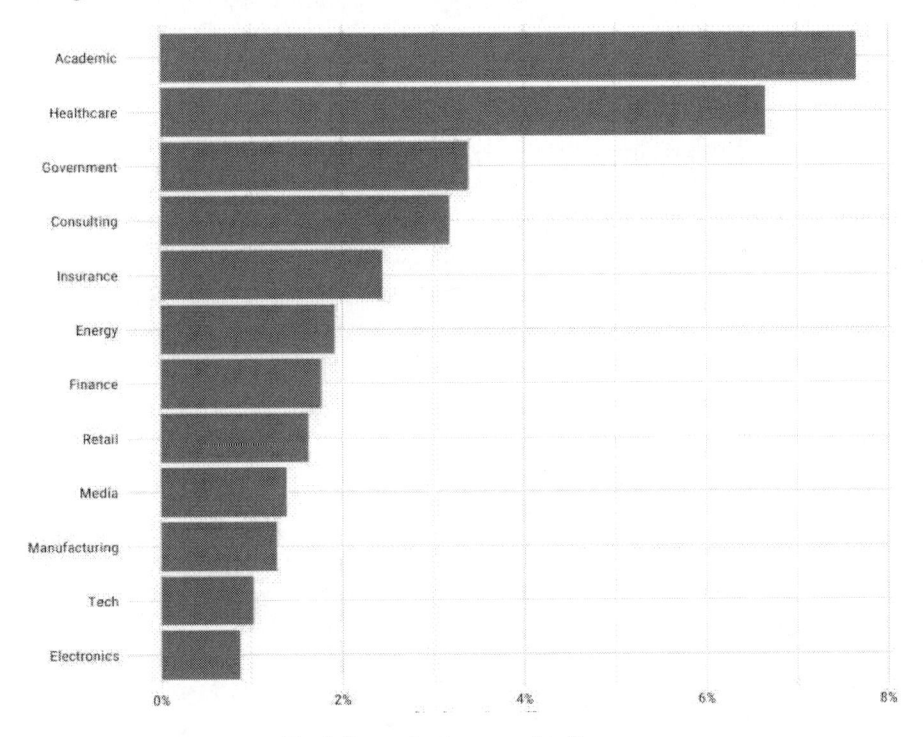

Fig.5. Recent business trend in R

Nowadays, various biomedical and healthcare tools like genomics, mobile biometric sensors, and smart-phone apps generate an enormous amount of knowledge. The combined pool of data from healthcare organizations and biomedical researchers has resulted in a better outlook, determination, and treatment of various diseases. This has helped in building an intelligent better and healthier personalized healthcare framework[26] using R as shown in figure 6.

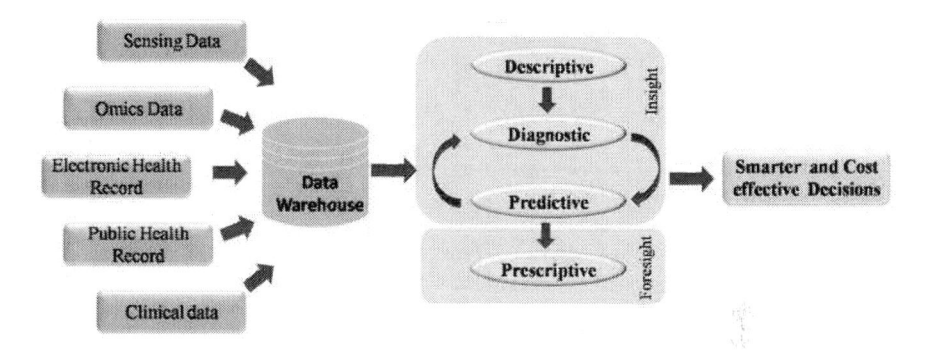

Fig.6. Healthcare Data Analytics using R

Working with structured Electronic Health Records (HER) data requires a mix of computational and statistical expertise. The rEHR package[27] greatly simplifies and accelerates the extraction and processing of coded data from EHR databases, enabling researchers to spend longer on their analyses, time that might rather be consumed with laborious preparation of research-ready data. The workflow is simple , amounting to a flat series of function calls instead of a fancy set of nested loops, therefore errors are far more easily spotted and stuck.

CHAPTER-4: Augmented and Virtual Reality in Medical Diagnosis

Virtual Reality (VR) means the user could watch and interact through the VR device but all the pictures displayed are "fake", which are all virtual. Augmented Reality (AR) known to be a virtual object that's generated by a computer through the important environment seen by a mobile, tablet or AR glasses. Mixed reality is located between the real environment and the virtual environment. Health care workers are commonly checking the patients' conditions through the computer on the mobile medical cart, VR, AR and MR technologies are gaining more and more attention in the healthcare field. Other than improving the inconvenience of traditional medical practices and education, it can also increase the effectiveness and efficiency of nursing and medical health care services. However, there are still some technical problems have yet to be overcome. Such as the mixing of the nursing and medical health care data system, the clarity and determination of the display image, the sturdiness of hardware, etc. Nowadays, there are many academics, medical institutions and manufacturers are developing some new techniques in order to overcome some related technical problems[28].

Virtual Reality (VR) and Augmented Reality (AR) represent huge potential for advances in diagnosis, treatment, therapy, and education. AR and VR can bring medical treatment and diagnoses across long distances, but the consideration for telemedicine needs to include a definition of where the doctor's office and patient's home are separated. The VR and AR technologies can help with better diagnoses and improved outcomes for patients, among other benefits. With the power of AR-VR, medical tech plays a key role in medical diagnosis. It has been advancing with the applications of latest technologies. These technologies can help with better diagnoses and improved outcomes for patients, among other benefits.

Advances in imaging technology over the previous couple of decades have made leaps within the effective diagnosis of medical conditions. Technologies such as MRIs and X-Rays have been helpful for allowing doctors to quickly make a diagnosis, the two-dimensional images they display have been limiting. AR is being utilized to project real-time medical data from an ultrasound directly onto the body of a patient, which the attending doctors can see with a headset. VR is being looked at as a way to literally transform the hospital or doctor's office into anywhere that it needs to be for the patient, a potential way to reduce anxiety. VR experiences can function adjunctive care with other treatment regimens, like programs that provide visuals for amputees or stroke patients in physiotherapy. Virtual reality headsets help to create immersive experiences, which can take them back to places they have been familiar. Smartphone applications are differently that VR and AR are being introduced to assist with patient therapy. Medical education traditionally involved many textbooks, and therefore the use of models or dissections to find out about the physical body and the way it works. Fujitsu has developed a VR heart simulator as shown in figure 7, which develop to enhance student understanding of a heart through three-dimensional, 360-degree observation of the structure. There is huge potential to set up digital "patients" through AR or VR, allowing students to diagnose and treat patients, and follow through with outcomes, without putting any living person at risk[29].

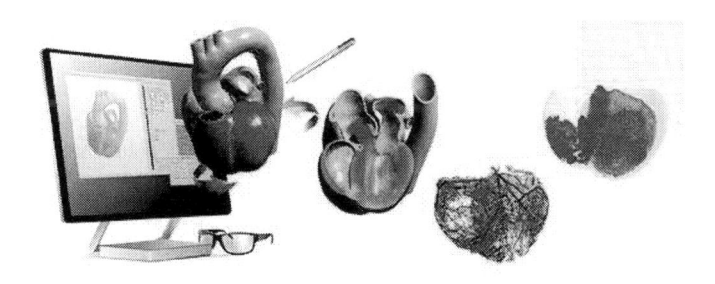

Fig.7. VR heart simulator

Patients are going to be ready to see for themselves the complexity of "excitation propagation," a phenomenon whereby electric stimulation from pacemaker cells spreads throughout a heart, with a stereoscopic, 360-degree view utilizing VR, allowing them to know how electrocardiograms are created through this process. Fujitsu has prepared simulation models recreating conditions like cardiac infarction, which enables students to review the differences in excitation propagation between a traditional heart and a diseased heart. By providing a stereoscopic view with VR, this technology supports the efficient teaching of medical students, enabling them to actually see such factors because the interrelation between the graph shown on the electrocardiogram and therefore the propagation of electrical signals, and also the difference between the behaviors of a heart both in normal times and when diseased. The heart simulator, developed by Fujitsu and Tokyo University, was generated using the K computer or a PC cluster, supported actual images of hearts took MRI and CT scans, accurately simulating the activity of a heart from the muscle fiber level. Fujitsu[29] has not only prepared models of healthy hearts, but simulated data of various heart diseases, including myocardial infarction, fatal arrhythmias, and left bundle branch blocks, enabling students to learn by comparing them with the activity of a traditional heart. Fujitsu will continue development of a greater kind of heart simulation models in light of the experience gained from this lecture, with the goal of offering this heart simulator viewer as educational software purchasable to educational and medical institutions during fiscal 2017.

New AR innovations can help enhance doctors and surgeons ability to diagnose, treat, and perform surgery on their patients more accurately by giving them access to real-time data and patient information faster, and more precisely than ever before. As data access technologies are already very advanced, the step is to supply real-time, life-saving patient information to surgeons which they will use during simple or complex procedures. Before using AR, these surgeons had to use a handheld scanner to locate major blood vessels near the wound, but their augmented reality system helps them find those major blood vessels directly and accurately by displaying them during a three-dimensional reflection. Bioflight[30] features a VR/AR doctor training, 360 ° enhanced videos to assist physicians as shown in figure 8, and surgeons study new products and procedures within their field. The company has developed an AR/VR a medical training module to help students and doctors refine their learn and increase their retention. Medical students could have access to practice procedures much earlier in their training careers than they might normally do, creating a brand new and unique learning opportunity. Augmedix[31] provides a technology-enabled documentation service for doctors and health systems, so physicians do not need to check their computers during patient visits, while medical notes are still generated in real time. Augmedix turns natural doctor-patient conversation into medical charts in real time, in order that doctors can specialise in what matters most – patient care. The idea for using AR in education is to simulate patient and surgical encounters for college students to create all of their mistakes on AR instead of during a dissection lab or worse, in a real-life procedure. Students will use AR in order that they can accurately study diagnosing patients with health conditions or participate in an AR surgery. Medical students have always based medicine on theory and proven evidence, and AR technologies allow them to visualize and practice those theories during their training. Through the utilization of AR to help in surgery, during the training of medical students, and even during regular doctor appointments.[32]

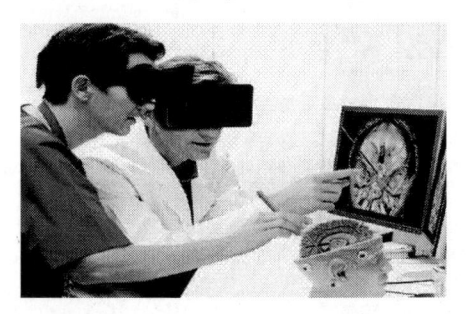

Fig.8. 360 ° enhanced videos to assist physicians

AR denotes a technique to combine real-world and virtual objects which are artificially generated digital content by a computer. As another aspect of AR is a registration between the real world and virtual objects, it aims to estimate a three-dimensional (3D) position of virtual objects related to the real world. The figure 9 shows the surgical navigation of two switchable systems, a resection margin calculated from a reconstructed 3D spinal tumor model and a captured scene for spinal tumor AR navigation. To improve the depth perception, an integrated VR and AR system was proposed that displayed in a very single window with aligned view axes and provided the gap between surgical instruments and target organs. AR system configuration The proposed VR and AR switchable surgical navigation system consists of position tracking and visualization sections[33]. A few advanced sorts of research have far and away proved that VR has better performance in detection diagnosis of varied diseases using VR imaging and planning techniques.

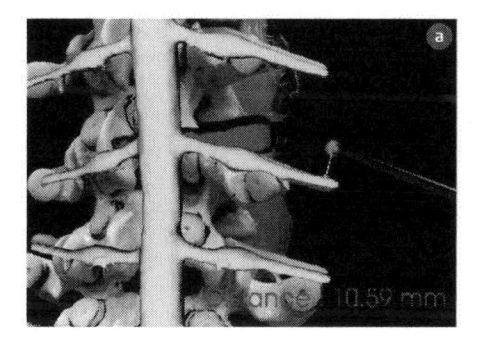

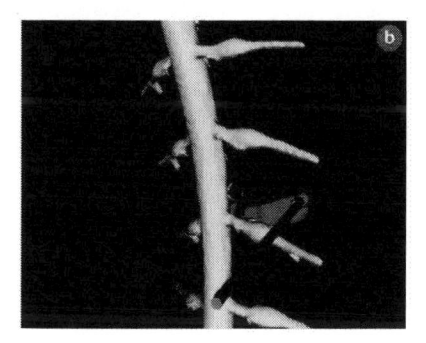

Fig.9. Spinal tumor: a) AR model and b) VR model

The future/ speculation of AR and VR[34]

- ✓ With the rise in medical imaging operations, plenty of oncology specialists are adopting digital reality technologies like AR and VR since there's enormous potential across different stages such as detection, diagnosis, and treatment.
- ✓ Considering this potential of VR/AR, healthcare may revolutionize the way the diagnostic practice is carried out to view MRI and CT images.
- ✓ There is a huge potential for AR and VR applications in medical imaging across its different stages namely detection, diagnosis and treatment.
- ✓ Considering the present advancement and maturity of VR/AR technologies, there are various ways during which these technologies will be applied to medical imaging operations: AR/VR are often used for tumor imaging during chemotherapy administration.
- ✓ Such AR/VR imaging applications can provide insights on changes in tumor size similarly as other details like end-to-end structure, shape, and margin.
- ✓ With current technologies in use, imaging provides two-dimensional information such as tumor location, laterality, distance, and size. This will help to know the structure of a posh tumor.
- ✓ There are some potential advantages with the utilization of AR/VR compared to most known volume rendering techniques in diagnostic imaging, which are listed below.
- ✓ The volume rendering technique takes tons more computer processing because it creates a man-made light within the image to get shadows for imaging.
- ✓ AR/VR imaging may decrease the number of manual thresholding by providing more details about complex structures.
- ✓ A radiologist, surgeon, and patient can improve their communication and collaboration with computer-generated graphics with this extra information.

- ✓ Such technology may allow a radiologist to deliver anatomical information quickly on the virtual surface and help them to grasp intimately by providing the potential of zooming a specific part of the virtual image.
- ✓ As AR/VR provides 3D imaging and there's an opportunity to deep dive with the potential of rotating, zooming and flying into a three-dimensional image with HMDs, there's a very high probability that the authors can detect tumor cells from the early stage which may remain unidentified with the current technologies and techniques.
- ✓ 3D augmented reality image may help a radiologist to deliver a transparent picture of the structural anomalies and provides a more accurate diagnosis.

CHAPTER-5: Application of AI in Medical Diagnosis

Machine Learning algorithms are implanted in every aspect of Artificial Intelligence, and below we describe the evolution of Machine Learning towards status as a general-purpose technology. It is claimed that artificial intelligence is playing a proposed Alan Turing (1950). This test was designed to an increasing role in the research of management science tests whether a particular machine can think or not. Artificial intelligence (AI) has been defined by Turing, the founding father of AI, as 'the science and engineering of creating intelligent machines, especially intelligent computer programs'. AI in health uses algorithms and software to approximate the cognition undertaken by human clinicians within the analysis of complex medical data. AI research has been divided into subfields, supported goals like machine learning or deep learning, and tools like neural networks, a subset of machine learning. AI has the potential to significantly transform the role of the doctor and revolutionize the practice of medicine, and it is important for all doctors, in particular those in positions of leadership within the health system, to anticipate the potential changes, forecast their impact and plan strategically for the medium to future [35].

From diagnosis and pathology to drug discovery and epidemiology, healthcare's reliance on large amounts of knowledge makes it one among the foremost exciting frontiers of AI Slowly but surely, AI is infiltrating almost every aspect of our lives. It is already busy within the background of the many routine tasks, powering virtual assistants like Siri and Alexa, recommendations from Amazon and Netflix, and underpinning billions of Google searches every day. However, the technology matures; AI's impact will become more profound, and nowhere is that more apparent than in healthcare.

Amazon Echo, Google Home, Siri[36] and therefore the myriad of other "assistants" that are out there are slowly but surely getting smarter and will , one day, be your doctor if researchers from New York University's Langone Medical Center have their way. According to new research, short voice clips are often wont to diagnose a range of diseases and conditions which suggests we just could be saving lives and catching diseases way sooner than we are currently. Prevention usually means money saved which interests plenty of various parties from billion-dollar industries like pharma, fitness, government services, and NGOs. Security and ownership will remain huge issues with something as personal as health and people's voices but perhaps there are opportunities attributable to the brands involved.

The field of AI gives the power to the machines to think analytically, using concepts. A tremendous contribution to the various areas has been made by Artificial Intelligence techniques from the last 2 decades. Artificial Intelligence will continue to play an increasingly important role in various fields. The concept of AI , areas of AI and therefore the AI techniques utilized, in the Network Intrusion Detection to protect the network from intruders. In the field of medicine, for medical image classification, within the accounting databases, and described how these AI techniques are utilized in computer games to resolve the common problems and to supply features to the games to have fun. There is a bright future in the analysis of Network Intrusion

Detection and there is also a definite future in the area of Power System Stabilizers. We conclude that further research in this area can be done as there are very promising and profitable results that are obtainable from such techniques. While scientists haven't yet realized the total potential and talent of AI. This technology and its applications will likely have far-reaching effects on human life within the years to return[37].

The implementation of Personalized Medicine heavily relies on AI algorithms[38]. However, it is still in its early stage, levels, and faces some challenges. While other problems such as research and implementation costs, and government regulations are challenges that are critical to the successful implementation of personalized medicine but not addressed by the algorithms discussed in this report. However, Personalized Medicine does not only faces challenges; it does pose some challenges further, such as; changing the medical community and practice to the extent that some futurist thinks algorithms and machines could replace most of the jobs doctors do today. Finally, the successful implementation of personalized medicine would save many lives and perfect the medical profession.

The thoughts about human perception versus digital data in a timeline further out than has been covered in this report. One of the major obstacles to be overcome in making health and health-care information useful is the gap between human cognition and digital data. Information concerning an individual patient is mostly obtained in forms designed to be accessible to medical personnel. Typical data may consist of X-ray or MRI or ultrasound pictures of the patient, visual records of heart or lung function varying with time, or verbal descriptions of the patient as seen by a nurse or a doctor. On the other hand, when data are stored in information systems and used, in medical research or to develop treatment guidelines, it is often reduced to statistical information, which is predominantly digital. The conversion of analog input into digital output is a burdensome task and may result in a loss of significant information that would have been helpful to the user. Now the scientists concentrate on how computer-based decision procedures, under the broad umbrella of artificial intelligence (AI), can assist in improving health and health care. Although advanced statistics and machine learning provide the inspiration for AI, there are currently revolutionary advances underway within the sub-field of neural networks. This has created tremendous excitement in many fields of science, including medicine and public health. First demonstrations have already emerged showing that deep neural networks can perform also because the best human clinicians in well-defined diagnostic tasks. In addition, AI-based tools are already appearing in health-oriented apps, which will be used on handheld, networked devices like smart-phones. The technology should address a big , identified clinical need. The technology must perform a minimum of similarly because the existing standard approach. Substantial clinical testing is required to verify the performance of the new technology under the wide selection of clinical situations during which it's going to be used. The new technology should provide improvements in patient outcomes, patient quality of life, practicality in use, and reduced medical system costs. The new technology is based on physical principles, rather than the less-understood correlations of AI, its review and acceptance process likely faced less skepticism than a new AI approach may encounter. For the medical profession to develop trust in AI-based tools, assessments a minimum of as rigorous are needed. In the US[39], a mixture of the Food and Drug Administration (FDA) regulations and clinical business models regulates adoptions of AI applications for clinical practice. For non-clinical personal smart device uses discussed in the following section, it will require public (user) confidence and may or may not require regulation.

Recent Application areas of AI:

- ✓ At the beginning of the system development, the hospital set up ten virtual patients' medical data to the trial and adjusted the clinical decision support system[40]. The prescription strategy of clinical doctors must consider many factors. To address this, we developed an individualized anti-diabetic medication recommendation system for patients with diabetes. Manually considering all possible conditions isn't only a waste of medical resources but also a burden on the system, to not mention that it's impractical. The AI system combines fuzzy logic and ontology reasoning, proposes an anti-diabetic medication recommendation system for patients with diabetes. It promotes a new concept of "patient-centered diabetes therapy." Anti-diabetic medications are recommended for the outpatients, and a useful ranking of medications is conducted. In addition to aiding doctors' clinical diagnosis, the system cannot only function a guide for doctors specializing in diabetes but also help family practitioners and interns in prescribing medications.

- ✓ Clinical decision-support apps[41] have huge potential to enhance access to care and quality of care. Clinical effectiveness trials are lacking, but the medical community may need to modernize its approach if it is to be truly committed to capitalizing on the opportunities of digitalization. Like all clinical tools, its user has an obligation to make sure its use is safe and appropriate for patients, particularly during this time where regulation is in its infancy.

- ✓ Informing clinical deciding through insights from past data is that the essence of evidence-based medicine. AI excels at well-defined tasks Research has focused on tasks where AI is in a position to effectively demonstrate its performance in reference to an individual's doctor. Patients cannot be expected to right away trust AI; a technology shrouded by mistrust. AI commonly handles tasks that are essential but limited enough in their scope so on leave initial responsibility of patient management with an individual's doctor. AI commonly handles tasks that are essential but limited enough in their scope soon leave the first responsibility of patient management with an individual's doctor." AI could automatically prepare the foremost important risks and actions given the patient's clinical record. Integrating these systems into clinical practice necessitates building a dependent relationship between AI and clinicians, where AI offers clinicians greater efficiency or cost-effectiveness and clinicians offer AI the essential clinical exposure it has to learn complex clinical case management[42].

- ✓ It is important that medical care physicians get better versed with the long run AI advances and also the new unknown territory the globe of medication is heading toward. The goal should be to strike a fragile interdependent balance between effective use of automation and AI and therefore the human strengths and judgment of trained medical care physicians. This is essential because AI completely replacing humans within the field of medication may be a concern, which could otherwise hamper the advantages, which may be derived from it.

CHAPTER-6: Blockchain in Medical Diagnosis

The current methods of medication contain traditional paper-based methods. The more advanced technology adopted to supply more coordinated health care. Blockchain could be a secure, decentralized online ledger that would be accustomed manages electronic health records (EHRs) efficiently[43], with the potential to enhance health outcomes by creating a conduit for interoperability. What strategies are proposed or trialed to implement a blockchain or blockchain for the management of electronic medical records, and the way do they improve efficiency compared to currently employed medical record management methods?

The application of blockchain could be improved interoperability and reduced long-term administrative costs would cause improved health outcomes. Efficiency of blockchain is either improved interoperability or cost-effectiveness, or improved health outcomes because of these.

A smart contract[44] is a computer protocol that runs automatically when the prerequisites are met, and it is an entity separate from the original blockchain technology. Many aspects of blockchain technology, like the immutability of the information stored in an exceedingly blockchain, are drawing the eye of the healthcare sector, and rosy prospects for several available cases are being discussed[45]. Blockchain technology is predicted to enhance medical history management and therefore the claim process, accelerate clinical and biomedical research and advance biomedical and healthcare data ledger. These expectations are based on the key aspects of blockchain technology, such as decentralized management, immutable audit trail, data provenance, robustness, and improved security and privacy. Medical data should be possessed, operated, and allowed to be utilized by data subjects apart from hospitals. This is a key concept of patient-centered interoperability that differs from conventional institution-driven interoperability. There are many challenges arising from patient-centered interoperability, such as data standards, security, and privacy, in addition to technology-related issues, such as scalability and speed, incentives, and governance. Blockchain technology can facilitate the transition from institution-driven interoperability to patient-centered interoperability. Blockchain technology allows patients to assign access rules for his or her medical data, for instance, permitting specific researchers to access parts of their data for a hard and fast period. Patients can connect to other hospitals and collect their medical data automatically. These functions, which may be implemented with blockchain technology, could also be useful for ensuring the rights of knowledge subjects as defined by the EU General Data Protection Regulation[46]. Blockchain technology is continually improving instead of completed, and it's several potential challenges that has to be addressed for it to be adopted for biomedical and healthcare applications.

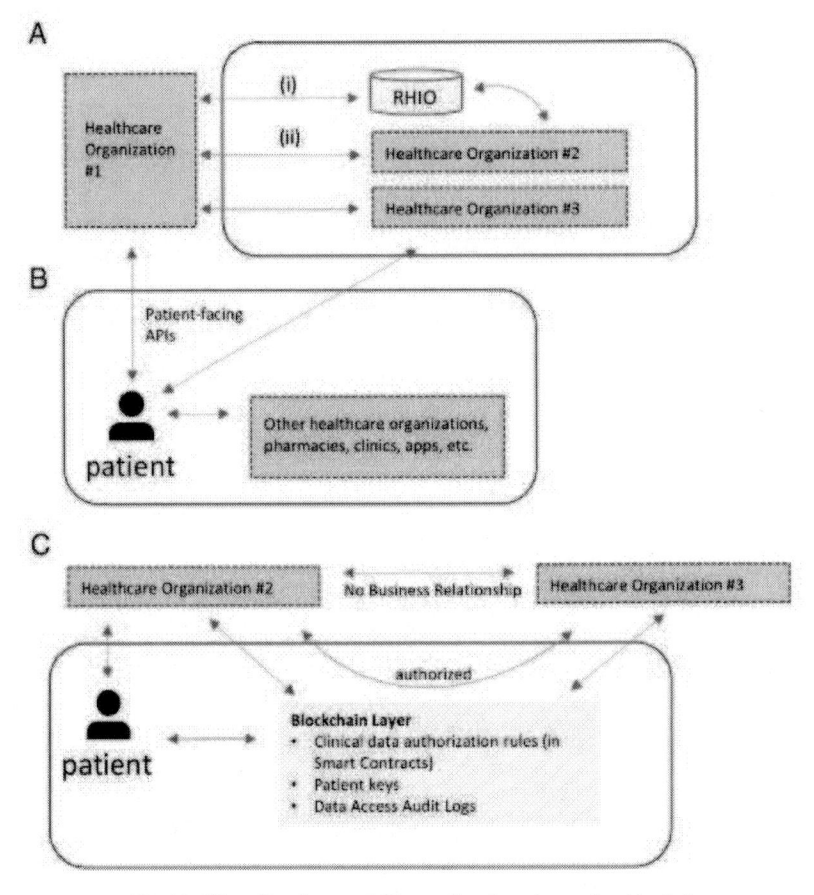

Fig.10. View, Retrieve and Share of patient data using blockchan.

Interoperability in healthcare has traditionally been focused around data exchange between business entities, for instance, different hospital systems. The healthcare interoperability landscape is usually centered around business entities, like hospitals, private clinics, and pharmacies, and data is usually created and silted within the knowledge system that makes it. The data may still be largely generated in institutional silos, but, patients will have the ability to build a comprehensive view of their health, retrieving their data and sharing it as appropriate with other entities depicted in figure 10[47].

Interoperability in healthcare is usually focused around data exchange between business entities—for example, multiple hospital systems through a state-wide Health Information

Exchange (HIE). The patient can still retrieve data directly from organization #2; through blockchain-enabled smart contracts, the patient can authorize the sharing of clinical EHR data between organization #2 and organization #3, which do not have a formal business relationship. The blockchain layer stores these authorization rules, alongside patient public keys, also as data access audit logs. The first-way blockchain technology could improve patient-driven interoperability is through the management of digital access rules.

Patients can manage their public keys—perhaps through an identity multi-sig wallet or mobile device—and use the public-key infrastructure (PKI) to establish their identity for retrieving clinical data from the blockchain, as well as adding new information. Second-Way blockchain technology could foster patient-driven interoperability is through data availability. Rapid access to clinical information may be a third major way blockchain technology could improve interoperability within the patient context. Institution-driven interoperability is that patients are not responsible for securing or storing their data—that is left to the entity generating the data. Moving patients to the middle of interoperability—even if they're authorizing release on behalf of the entities—has the potential to shift actual data governance faraway from institutions, for interfaced data not primarily generated by the entity. Blockchain could provide an important catalyst for improving data exchange, for patient-driven interoperability. Blockchain implementations that allow for selective disclosure of private information and rely on zero-knowledge cryptography to provide verification of transactions with a high degree of privacy over the underlying data will be needed within the healthcare industry as shown in figure 11[48].

In spite of the very fact that healthcare, once during a while, lingers behind different ventures in receiving new advancements, thanks to the integrity of the potential data, there could also be motivation to understand blockchain in healthcare within the near future. Managing electronic health records within the blockchain could have a couple of focal points.

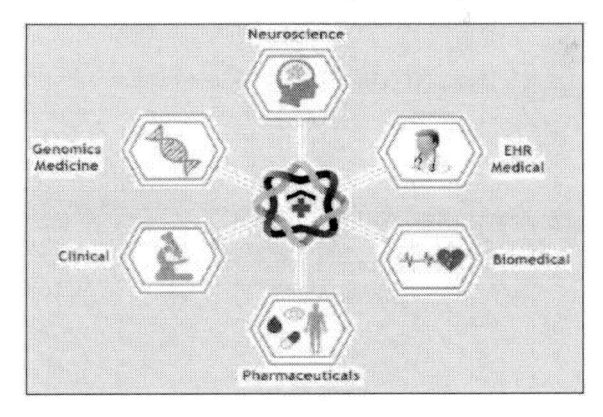

Fig.11. Application of blockchan in Healtcare.

The discussed application of smart contracts encourages us to adopt them, to require care of each minor and significant exchange within the healthcare industry. Smart contracts would give an unbreakable chain of blocks that might take into consideration-individualized care without breaking into clinical frameworks. Converging clinical systems, through a blockchain smart contract, would resist the assembly of any duplicate copy within the parent-centralized system. The potential assistance of blockchain for researchers is that it could provide verified and time stamped versions of scientific studies. Just as if the smart contracts allow patients to regulate their data, a documentation blockchain record would allow researchers to possess a sustainable history of their findings. In the giant field of the pharmaceutical industry, blockchain may be a must-have technology. The opportunities and challenges of blockchain application[48] is shown in figure 12.

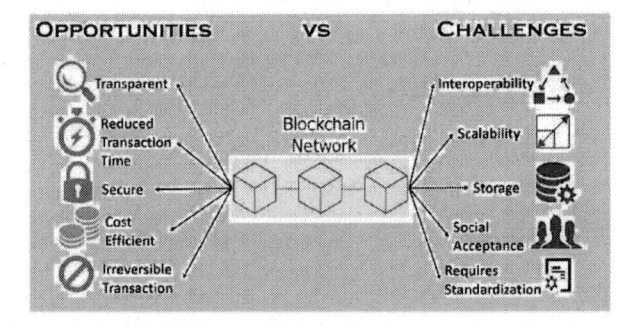

Fig.12. Opportunities and challenges of blockchain.

CHAPTER-7: 3D Printing in Healthcare

Artificial intelligence has transformed the way we do business and our everyday lives. Virtual assistants, computer-aided diagnosis and clinical decision support are just a couple of samples of how AI in healthcare has transformed the world. 3D printing is employed extensively in healthcare, whether in terms of making customized prosthetics, implants, tissue and organ fabrication[49]. The 3D printing is great for the manufacturing industry; the healthcare industry was just starting to consider the potential the new technology could provide. It is anticipated the use of 3D technologies will grow by as much as 21% over the decade in the healthcare industry. Hospitals and physicians have printed different types of medical devices and implants on 3D printers. Other potential uses for 3D printer technologies are starting to be researched, like printing prosthetics and living tissue, organs, and artificial bones. Augmented reality isn't identical thing as Virtual-Reality (VR), another emerging technology within the healthcare industry. Aside from exploring 3D printing technologies for printing medications and medical devices as shown in figure 13, pharmaceuticals are tapping into existing and emerging technologies to help speed up the research and development of new medications and devices[50]. That is why Artificial intelligence (AI), robotics and 3D printing have progressed rapidly.

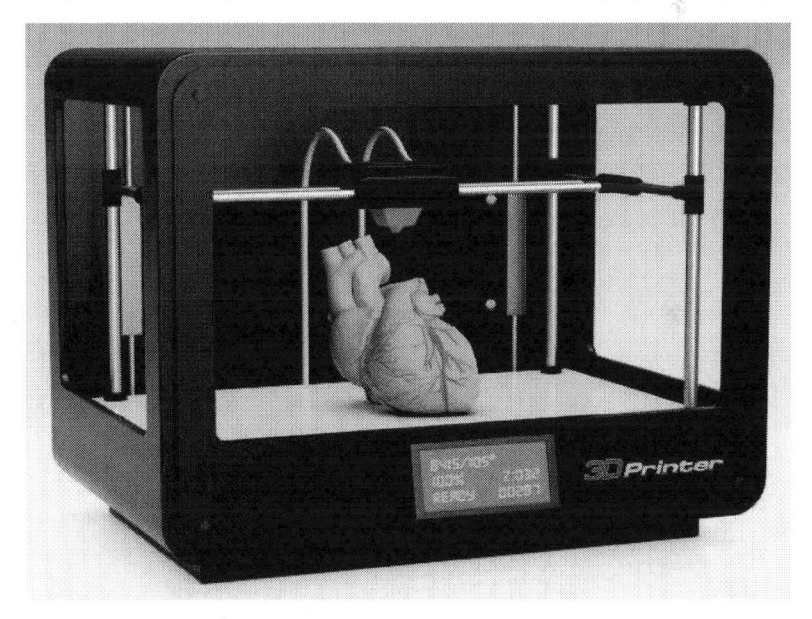

Fig.13. 3D Printer printed Artificial Heart.

A lack of surgical planning leads to longer surgery times, an absence of clarity among surgical teams, higher costs to the healthcare provider, and potentially a worse outcome for the patient. The algorithms developed by axial3D[51] are accustomed streamline the method of turning medical images into 3D-printed models to guide surgical planning. With the advent of fast and easy access to 3D printing, requests for 3D prints are made directly through axial3D's online portal, axial3Dinsight, where the combination of automated segmentation, expert engineers and rapid 3D printing mean axial3D can return a patient-specific 3D printed model within 48 hours. Axial3D produced a model within 24 hours, and using this, the surgical team identified small bone fragments not visible on the images, resulting in the team deciding the original plan needed to change significantly. This resulted within the surgery duration being reduced by approximately 3 hours and an improved outcome for the patient. Without the knowledge obtained from the 3D model, we might have planned one posterior approach and therefore the surgical reduction is not possible as a result, this saved significant operative time.

The effect of technological and medical advances in the architectural design of future healthcare facilities can highly be expected as follows[52]:

- ✓ Future hospitals will be fully robotic.
- ✓ AI and robots will do nearly all procedures, from electronic registration (e-healthcare) to diagnosis (AI) to surgery (by a robot, not a human).
- ✓ 3D printers will be placed in hospitals to produce almost everything, from medical equipment to human body parts, like artificial ears.
- ✓ AI will be used to diagnose, eliminating the need for MRIs and another scan.
- ✓ The use of telecare and E-healthcare will mean shorter waiting times for patients and less space needed for waiting areas.
- ✓ Telecare and E-healthcare will allow patients to remain at home rather than stay in a hospital, eliminating the need for more hospital beds.
- ✓ 3D printing will be used to produce medicine, eliminating the need for pharmacies; patients will be able to download their prescriptions which are obtained by AI, print his/her medication by 3D printer, and then receive it in a favorite place.
- ✓ Computer chips placed in every human body will allow all diseases to be diagnosed at an early stage; all the health information of each individual will be readily available.
- ✓ Large- and small-scale decentralization in hospitals and healthcare facilities may lead to a different architectural layout than current trends.
- ✓ Robotic systems are already used for a few surgeries, and other prototypes are being explored. To maintain safe and effective robotic surgery, surgeons must still design evidence-based pathways to the credentialing of robotic surgical teams. Despite the small number of studies from several single centers and a handful of surgeons, the results show good intra-operative results with robotic surgery. In the near future, all surgeries are going to be done by robots.
- ✓ While it is unlikely that AI will entirely replace physicians, it can assist in many ways.

Reference

[1] M. Pignone and R. Salazar, "Disease Prevention & Health Promotion," in *Current Medical Diagnosis & Treatment 2019*, M. A. Papadakis, S. J. McPhee, and M. W. Rabow, Eds. New York, NY: McGraw-Hill Education, 2019.
[2] P. L. Nadler and R. Gonzales, "Common Symptoms," in *Current Medical Diagnosis & Treatment 2019*, M. A. Papadakis, S. J. McPhee, and M. W. Rabow, Eds. New York, NY: McGraw-Hill Education, 2019.
[3] H. Q. Cheng, "Preoperative Evaluation & Perioperative Management," in *Current Medical Diagnosis & Treatment 2019*, M. A. Papadakis, S. J. McPhee, and M. W. Rabow, Eds. New York, NY: McGraw-Hill Education, 2019.
[4] C. M. Lu, "Diagnostic Testing & Medical Decision Making," in *Current Medical Diagnosis & Treatment 2019*, M. A. Papadakis, S. J. McPhee, and M. W. Rabow, Eds. New York, NY: McGraw-Hill Education, 2019.
[5] *Read "Improving Diagnosis in Health Care" at NAP.edu.* .
[6] T. Syzek, "The Diagnostic Process: Rediscovering the Basic Steps," 2019. [Online]. Available: https://blog.thesullivangroup.com/rsqsolutions/diagnostic-process-rediscovering-basic-steps. [Accessed: 24-Nov-2019].
[7] S. Das, M. K. Sanyal, and D. Datta, "Artificial Intelligent Reliable Doctor (AIRDr.): Prospect of Disease Prediction Using Reliability," in *Intelligent Computing Paradigm: Recent Trends*, vol. 784, J. K. Mandal and D. Sinha, Eds. Singapore: Springer Singapore, 2020, pp. 21–42.
[8] S. Das, M. K. Sanyal, D. Datta, and A. Biswas, "AISLDr: Artificial Intelligent Self-learning Doctor," in *Intelligent Engineering Informatics*, vol. 695, V. Bhateja, C. A. Coello Coello, S. C. Satapathy, and P. K. Pattnaik, Eds. Singapore: Springer Singapore, 2018, pp. 79–90.
[9] S. Das, M. K. Sanyal, and D. Datta, "Advanced Diagnosis of Deadly Diseases Using Regression and Neural Network," in *Social Transformation – Digital Way*, vol. 836, J. K. Mandal and D. Sinha, Eds. Singapore: Springer Singapore, 2018, pp. 330–351.
[10] J. A. Bullinaria, "IAI : The Roots, Goals and Sub-fields of AI," p. 16, 2005.
[11] "Artificial Intelligence Techniques in Medicine and Healthcare," 2019. [Online]. Available: http://what-when-how.com/medical-informatics/artificial-intelligence-techniques-in-medicine-and-healthcare/. [Accessed: 25-Dec-2019].
[12] "Artificial Intelligence in Medicine | The Top 4 Applications," 2019. [Online]. Available: https://www.datarevenue.com/en-blog/artificial-intelligence-in-medicine. [Accessed: 25-Dec-2019].
[13] Matthew Inkawhich, "Chatbot Tutorial — PyTorch Tutorials 1.3.1 documentation," 2019. [Online]. Available: https://pytorch.org/tutorials/beginner/chatbot_tutorial.html. [Accessed: 26-Dec-2019].
[14] E. Sandewall, "Ontology, Taxonomy and Type in Artificial Intelligence," p. 32.
[15] "What is an ontology and why we need it." [Online]. Available: https://protege.stanford.edu/publications/ontology_development/ontology101-noy-mcguinness.html. [Accessed: 26-Dec-2019].

[16] "Artificial Intelligence - foundations of computational agents -- 13.3 Ontologies and Knowledge Sharing." [Online]. Available: https://artint.info/html/ArtInt_316.html. [Accessed: 26-Dec-2019].

[17] Hamid R. Tizhoosh, "(4) (PDF) Artificial Intelligence and Digital Pathology: Challenges and Opportunities," *ResearchGate*. [Online]. Available: https://www.researchgate.net/publication/328934914_Artificial_Intelligence_and_Digital_Pathology_Challenges_and_Opportunities. [Accessed: 26-Dec-2019].

[18] M. Toussaint, "Artificial Intelligence First-Order Logic," p. 62, 2016.

[19] "3.1: First Order Logic Syntax and Semantics," *Engineering LibreTexts*, 18-Dec-2018. [Online]. Available: https://eng.libretexts.org/Bookshelves/Computer_Science/Book%3A_An_Introduction_to_Ontology_Engineering_(Keet)/03%3A_First_Order_Logic_and_Automated_Reasoning_in_a_Nutshell/3.01%3A_First_Order_Logic_Syntax_and_Semantics. [Accessed: 21-Feb-2020].

[20] A. Patel and S. Jain, "Formalisms of Representing Knowledge," *Procedia Computer Science*, vol. 125, pp. 542–549, 2018, doi: 10.1016/j.procs.2017.12.070.

[21] "Top 5 best Programming Languages for Artificial Intelligence field," *GeeksforGeeks*, 09-Nov-2017. [Online]. Available: https://www.geeksforgeeks.org/top-5-best-programming-languages-for-artificial-intelligence-field/. [Accessed: 26-Dec-2019].

[22] "SWI-Prolog -- Manual," 2020. [Online]. Available: https://www.swi-prolog.org/pldoc/man?section=quickstart. [Accessed: 21-Jan-2020].

[23] W. G. Wilson, "Prolog for applications programming," *IBM Syst. J.*, vol. 25, no. 2, pp. 190–206, 1986, doi: 10.1147/sj.252.0190.

[24] B. Di Martino, A. Esposito, S. Liguori, F. Ospedale, S. A. Maisto, and S. Nacchia, "A Fuzzy Prolog and Ontology Driven Framework for Medical Diagnosis Using IoT Devices," in *Complex, Intelligent, and Software Intensive Systems*, vol. 611, L. Barolli and O. Terzo, Eds. Cham: Springer International Publishing, 2018, pp. 875–884.

[25] "What is R Programming Language? Introduction & Basics." [Online]. Available: https://www.guru99.com/r-programming-introduction-basics.html. [Accessed: 11-Feb-2020].

[26] S. Dash, S. K. Shakyawar, M. Sharma, and S. Kaushik, "Big data in healthcare: management, analysis and future prospects," *Journal of Big Data*, vol. 6, no. 1, p. 54, Jun. 2019, doi: 10.1186/s40537-019-0217-0.

[27] D. A. Springate, R. Parisi, I. Olier, D. Reeves, and E. Kontopantelis, "rEHR: An R package for manipulating and analysing Electronic Health Record data," *PLOS ONE*, vol. 12, no. 2, p. e0171784, Feb. 2017, doi: 10.1371/journal.pone.0171784.

[28] J. J. Lee, "Preliminary Study of VR and AR Applications in Medical and Healthcare Education," *Journal of Nursing and Health Studies*, vol. 03, no. 01, 2018, doi: 10.21767/2574-2825.100030.

[29] "VR and AR for MedTech, the Latest! – Koombea Blog Post," *Koombea – Bringing apps to life*, 30-Jul-2018. [Online]. Available: https://www.koombea.com/blog/vr-and-ar-for-medtech/. [Accessed: 08-Feb-2020].

[30] "Bioflight VR Archives," *Touchstone Research*, 2020. [Online]. Available: https://touchstoneresearch.com/tag/bioflight-vr/. [Accessed: 08-Feb-2020].

[31] "Augmedix | McKesson and Augmedix Expand Collaboration to Enhance the Doctor-Patient Relationship," *Augmedix*, 2020. [Online]. Available: https://augmedix.com/updates/mckesson-and-augmedix-expand-collaboration-to-enhance-the-doctor-patient-relationship/. [Accessed: 08-Feb-2020].

[32] "Augmented Reality in Healthcare," *None*, 2020. [Online]. Available: https://www.plugandplaytechcenter.com/resources/augmented-reality-healthcare/. [Accessed: 08-Feb-2020].

[33] H.-G. Ha and J. Hong, "Augmented Reality in Medicine," *Hanyang Medical Reviews*, vol. 36, no. 4, p. 242, 2016, doi: 10.7599/hmr.2016.36.4.242.

[34] "The Future Role of Augmented Reality and Virtual Reality in Medical Imaging," 30-Apr-2018. [Online]. Available: https://www.einfochips.com/blog/the-future-role-of-augmented-reality-and-virtual-reality-in-medical-imaging/. [Accessed: 09-Feb-2020].

[35] E. Loh, "Medicine and the rise of the robots: a qualitative review of recent advances of artificial intelligence in health," *BMJ Leader*, vol. 2, no. 2, pp. 59–63, Jun. 2018, doi: 10.1136/leader-2018-000071.

[36] P. Armstrong, "Alexa, Cortana And Siri Are About To Diagnose Your Health," *Forbes*, 2020. [Online]. Available: https://www.forbes.com/sites/paularmstrongtech/2017/01/23/alexa-cortana-and-siri-are-about-to-diagnose-your-health/. [Accessed: 13-Feb-2020].

[37] A. Pannu, "Artificial Intelligence and its Application in Different Areas," vol. 4, no. 10, p. 6, 2015.

[38] J. Awwalu, A. G. Garba, A. Ghazvini, and R. Atuah, "Artificial Intelligence in Personalized Medicine Application of AI Algorithms in Solving Personalized Medicine Problems," *International Journal of Computer Theory and Engineering*, vol. 7, no. 6, pp. 439–443, Dec. 2015, doi: 10.7763/IJCTE.2015.V7.999.

[39] D. Derrington, "Artificial Intelligence for Health and Health Care," p. 69.

[40] R.-C. Chen, H. Q. Jiang, C.-Y. Huang, and C.-T. Bau, "Clinical Decision Support System for Diabetes Based on Ontology Reasoning and TOPSIS Analysis," *Journal of Healthcare Engineering*, 2017. [Online]. Available: https://www.hindawi.com/journals/jhe/2017/4307508/. [Accessed: 20-Feb-2020].

[41] H. A. Watson, R. M. Tribe, and A. H. Shennan, "The role of medical smartphone apps in clinical decision-support: A literature review," *Artificial Intelligence in Medicine*, vol. 100, p. 101707, Sep. 2019, doi: 10.1016/j.artmed.2019.101707.

[42] V. H. Buch, I. Ahmed, and M. Maruthappu, "Artificial intelligence in medicine: current trends and future possibilities," *Br J Gen Pract*, vol. 68, no. 668, pp. 143–144, Mar. 2018, doi: 10.3399/bjgp18X695213.

[43] A. A. Vazirani, O. O'Donoghue, D. Brindley, and E. Meinert, "Implementing Blockchains for Efficient Health Care: Systematic Review," *Journal of Medical Internet Research*, vol. 21, no. 2, p. e12439, 2019, doi: 10.2196/12439.

[44] "Smart contract," *Wikipedia*. 02-Feb-2020.

[45] "Blockchain in Healthcare Today (BHTY)'s page on Publons." [Online]. Available: https://publons.com/journal/91111/blockchain-in-healthcare-today-bhty. [Accessed: 27-Feb-2020].

[46] H.-J. Yoon, "Blockchain Technology and Healthcare," *Healthc Inform Res*, vol. 25, no. 2, pp. 59–60, Apr. 2019, doi: 10.4258/hir.2019.25.2.59.

[47] W. J. Gordon and C. Catalini, "Blockchain Technology for Healthcare: Facilitating the Transition to Patient-Driven Interoperability," *Computational and Structural Biotechnology Journal*, vol. 16, pp. 224–230, 2018, doi: 10.1016/j.csbj.2018.06.003.

[48] A. A. Siyal, A. Z. Junejo, M. Zawish, K. Ahmed, A. Khalil, and G. Soursou, "Applications of Blockchain Technology in Medicine and Healthcare: Challenges and Future

Perspectives," *Cryptography*, vol. 3, no. 1, p. 3, Jan. 2019, doi: 10.3390/cryptography3010003.

[49] L. Kim, Director, Privacy, Security, and HIMSS, "The Role of Artificial Intelligence in Healthcare and Society," 18-Jul-2019. [Online]. Available: https://www.himss.org/resources/role-artificial-intelligence-healthcare-and-society. [Accessed: 29-Feb-2020].

[50] "AI, Drones, 3D Printing: The Future of the Healthcare Industry," *A-Plus Corporation*, 22-Aug-2017. [Online]. Available: https://www.aplususapharma.com/blog/ai-drones-3d-printing-future-healthcare-industry/. [Accessed: 29-Feb-2020].

[51] "AI In Healthcare Use Case 38: axial3D," *Disruptor Daily*, 22-Jul-2019. [Online]. Available: https://www.disruptordaily.com/ai-in-healthcare-use-case-axial3d/. [Accessed: 29-Feb-2020].

[52] M. Vatandsoost and S. Litkouhi, "The Future of Healthcare Facilities: How Technology and Medical Advances May Shape Hospitals of the Future," *Hospital Practices and Research*, vol. 4, no. 1, pp. 1–11, Feb. 2019, doi: 10.15171/hpr.2019.01.

Made in the USA
Columbia, SC
21 May 2021